WAITING FOR THE MIST TO CLEAR

WAITING FOR THE MIST TO CLEAR

Kinsman Clive

Book Guild Publishing
Sussex, England

First published in Great Britain in 2012 by
The Book Guild Ltd
Pavilion View
19 New Road
Brighton, BN1 1UF

Typesetting in Bembo by
Nat-Type, Cheshire

Printed and Bound in Great Britain by
CPI Group (UK) Ltd, Croydon, CR0 4YY

A catalogue record for this book is available from
The British Library.

ISBN 978 1 84624 736 1

In loving memory of Pamela Anne Tupman (Pam), the Author's life-long close friend and his secretarial aide for many years. Pam encouraged his writing and always urged him to publish his poetry. Pam was instrumental in his being awarded an MBE. Sadly Pam died in 2008. Her ashes are interred at All Saints' Church, Sutton Bingham, Somerset.

Contents

Foreword

The Author, Brian Rousell, MBE, because there are so many pronunciations and spellings of his surname, writes under a pseudonym, Kinsman Clive. Kinsman was the maiden name of the grandmother of a man he knew in his twenties, whose work for the community and endless charitable causes left a lasting impression on him. Clive because if he had had a son, he would have been called Clive.

The Author is a history man, a romantic. His great passion is the beautiful, peaceful little Norman church, All Saints', Sutton Bingham, Somerset, 1111–2011, nine hundred years old and still very much alive. Besides the British Isles, it has visitors from all over the world and more especially Australia and North America. On 25th November, 1997 he was invested by Her Majesty, the Queen, at Buckingham Palace, as an MBE, for his services to All Saints' and his other charitable interests.

He has had to cope with serious illness all his life. He had little education. He suffers from severe hereditary sight and hearing loss. Labyrinthitis means his balance is poor. He is prone, without warning, to bouts of giddiness and nausea. He has worn hearing aids for 35 years. He has lost all his natural hearing. Corneal dystrophy, band degeneration, means he has survived 16 major eye surgeries in the last twenty-two years, including five corneal grafts. He became totally blind in his right eye in 1996. A pressure valve in his left eye helps to control complex glaucoma. Although he strains every day to hear and see, he is grateful to medical science for the limited sight and hearing he still retains. Without the dedicated, unstinting help of kindly medical and nursing teams, he would be totally blind and without hearing. He must mention the hospitals concerned. They are Dorchester, East Grinstead, Moorfields and St. Thomas's London, Salisbury, Southampton and Yeovil.

The Author's wife, Pauline, was the most gifted person he has ever known. She attended University College, London and the world famous Slade School of Art. She was a brilliant artist, teacher, gardener. Everything she touched in her life turned to gold. Her end was tragic. She suffered from severe dementia, Lewy Body disease, for eleven years. An old friend of hers and fellow university student said to the Author one day: 'You are a rare couple to have so much to leave behind, Pauline's paintings and your writing.'

Urged by his family and friends, he has agreed to publish some of his poetry. He is keen that any resultant publicity will help to raise the profile of the Dorset Blind Association with which he has been involved for about 20 years. It is a dedicated, enterprising unit which embraces the care of those suffering from blindness, partial sight and deafness, throughout the County of Dorset and beyond.

Writing

... Is like watching an elderly man leaning on a walking stick, strolling around a cricket ground during the interval. A piece of paper blows in front of him. He stabs it with his stick. If he misses, it is gone.

As thoughts cross your path, unless they can be held with pen to paper, they are lost.

Grammar

Beware the split infinitive
or the inflection of the word.

Always remember
        with what
not
        what with.

Never
        stop fool
but
        full stop!

The Sea

The sea!
The giant sea!
Its ebb and flow
      is all we know.
What is it thinking?

So gentle,
yet so fierce
      as it crashes
            across the strand
and invades the land,
      bringing fear ... and death.
What is it thinking?

It is our friend
when, with bucket and spade,
      days have no end.
This morning it was far away,
      now it comes near.
We are told to wish it goodbye
      until ... next year.
What is it thinking?

It is time to go
We must hurry
      but we dawdle
            as we prepare
and watch the sea
    lapping a lonely deck chair.
What is it thinking?

Seascape

A Cornish inlet,
reluctant swell
and idling surf
until
they are whipped
by the wind in its fury.

A Country Lane

It winds
    and winds again
    and takes no heed of speed.
It does not care
    for race and tear
    because ...
        tomorrow ...
    it will still be there
    in Dorset.

Happiness à la Australian Chardonnay

Clad in her butcher's apron,
        she cooked a perfect meal
        of prawns, mushrooms and rice.
His enquiry was answered by, 'Stirfry'!
It opened his eyes
        to a new cuisine
        enjoyed with Australian Chardonnay.

In the lounge,
        he lay on a settee,
        content …
She joined him,
resting her back on his chest,
        so they could both watch the sunset
        of this glorious late summer day.

Chardonnay is close to hand.
Curtains, not drawn,
        dusk steals the light …
In the darkness …
        they sip from one glass.
Chardonnay's warmth adds to their happiness.
They enjoy the summer night,
        speaking in murmurs and whispers …
        some of the time …

The New Year

The biting wind blows between
      the bars of the gate
      which leads to the New Year.
Its cruel spikes are tipped with ice.

I know what the new year
      holds for me.
Much, much sadness, little joy.
More blind, more deaf, more pain.
Will I see a Christmas tree again
      or hear the two absorbing passions of my life?
Music and the gentle voice
      she brought from her continent
      which gives me the will to live.

The gate closes behind me.
There is no escape.
I must accept the challenge
      of each bewildering day.
Yesterday will be quickly cast aside
      but its agony will haunt the memory.

Hardraw Force Waterfall, North Yorkshire

Gentle silence except for the sound
of falling water
and birds preparing for bed.

Captivating, spellbinding silence
as October afternoon
gives way to twilight
and then to dusk.

An Autumn leaf floated in a quiet pool,
desperately trying to come to terms
with its new surroundings ...
then trespassed, unwisely, into the current
and was carried away ...
until, the end of time?

Her gentleness is overwhelming.
He is alive again!
Apart from his family
he lives only for her.
They exchange the same greeting,
'I love you!'

They hug ever closer
despite fleece and walking boots.
It is a golden moment in the gentle silence
of an October afternoon ...

The Next Morning

There is a challenge
     in the empty room,
the heavy curtains
     shut out the gloom.
The embers of the fire
     still glow
and empty glasses
     gleam,
          but stay silent.
Stale cigar smoke
     clings to holly
          and mistletoe
          which must go
          as another year
        of toil begins.

Nightingale

Everything is still.
Curtains: hastened from windows
        already flung wide,
        greet the Diva
        of a Summer night.

She sings so clear
        it holds the ear.
Her time is short
        as dusk is close to dawn.

A yawn is disregarded.
Eyes stay wide
        'til nightingale falls silent.
Such magic has kept
        her captive audience
        spellbound.

Frustration and tensions
        have flown.
Tranquil we lie,
        waiting …
        to greet the day …
        refreshed.

In Passing

Those of you
that follow us
who survived
without any fuss …
although …
some of our minds
and bodies
were badly broken.

Remember … Armistice
At the 11th on the 11th of the 11th
All your lives!

In September Sunshine

Flags fly at half-mast,
in September sunshine.

The Abbey Bell tolls the minutes away,
in September sunshine.

Horse shoes chatter,
in September sunshine.

Gun carriage rumbles,
in September sunshine.

Guardsmen's boots begin their slow tread,
in September sunshine.

Petals pave the way,
in September sunshine.

Heads are bowed,
in September sunshine.

Tears well and trickle slowly down, unheeded,
in September sunshine.

Stranger holds the hand of stranger,
in September sunshine.

Vows of caring and kindness are renewed,
in September sunshine.

We all grieve,
in September sunshine,
yet our hearts have never been so warm.

Sixty Years Ago (1940–2000)

I was ten.
The gods of war
bestowed much cruelty.
We were nearly lost.
Were we?
Then the challenge ...
'I have nothing to offer you.'
Instinctively, we knew
   he would see us through.

In our villages.
   Safe a-bed,
     Still we lie.

Our gratitude must extend
   through our children's children
   and beyond ... for without
     Winston Churchill
      we would die
    Sixty years ago.

Speedy Recovery

I am so very *ill*.
They say I am
at death's door
and have gone
to get the key.

What!
I am not hanging about.
I am impatient
to get better!

Rubicon

He holds her voice and laughter
       in his head …
       until the telephone rings again.
They had yet to hold hands
       but they were crossing together.

Anglers' Lodge

November!
Closed season.

Clear morning.
Brilliant sun.
Every blade of grass
      is weighed down with
      frost's sparkling armour.

A stillness came
      with the morning wake.
Although everything is sharp,
      the countryside.
      lies sleeping.

She ... *beautiful creature,*
      is leaning on the veranda rail.
Captivated ...
      by the lakeside scene.
He ...
      watches and waits ...
      for her inviting smile ...

Dull November?

September Pilgrimage

Dawn; high noon and setting sun,
tinge the spray
from the Horseshoe Falls
with gentle hues.

Unaided by human hand,
the flow of the black water
of the Niagara River
quickens its pace
as if ordered by
the Giant Gravity
who hurtles it over the precipice.

It falls in white sparkling cascades
backed by beautiful,
colourful turquoise cushions.

Compelling, fascinating …
Completely absorbing
to the human mind.
Can it be real …?
It shouts back
with its thunderous voice.
'Yes. I am real.
I have been alive and well
for millions of years
and shall continue so
until the end of time.'

'Listen to me …
Take one raindrop.
Magnify it billions of times.
Find me a precipice,
then …
I will show you
what I can do … !'

September's Legacy

Amid tranquil days and meaner nights
        when migrant birds prepare for flight,
dawn sleeps later every day
        and dusk is never far away.

Days of Summer's glory linger,
overgrown and over-burdened
        with such a luscious store.

Wasps feed voraciously as though aware
        of an unseen danger.
They fall, stupefied and angry.
The sting in the tail of the mellow season.

Unlike the brief morning lick of Summer,
Autumn's dew clings as if to warn
        of the need to wear stouter shoes or boots.

The electric blanket, shunned all Summer long,
suddenly becomes a coveted, comforting companion.
Soon, General Heating
        will assemble his troops in every room.
Although an essential safeguard,
        they are viewed with disdain.
Their pay will certainly rise again this year.

They will remain at their post until well into the Spring.
Slowly but surely eating away at the precious stockpile,
        carefully laid on one side to pay for the Summer holiday.

Bliss

The grass needs cutting again.
Dead-heading is a daily necessity.
The pool and its filter
      have had their Summer clean.
The cascade chuckles happily.
Goldfish rush about
      as if on time trials
      for their Summer Olympics,
stopping only at feeding time
      to nuzzle fingertips!

We cling to the long July evenings
      enjoying the still, warm twilight,
... without a cardigan ...
before August, brings that
      first hint of Autumn ...

Hanging baskets of trailing fuschias
      accommodate honeysuckle.
Its perfume arrests the nostrils
      and invades the mind ...
Everything is Peace.

Portent

Harsh white muslin
      will soon return
      to drape the hill
      and sparkle with
      devilish glee in the
      ageing Summer sun
      which rises with
      increasing lethargy.

The noon of Summer
      was so brief …
and now;
sunset takes us unaware
      and dawn is far away.

Mornings can be disturbed
      to see the sun
      restrained by leaden cloud
      when breezes laze
      in the doldrums
      and take no heed
      of the sun's misery.

Surely …
Spring will return?
Meanwhile …
Autumn's gorgeous cloak
      is our cushion, until
      the hard hand of Winter
      descends to crush the spirit.

School Holiday

The grandchildren have come to stay!
The guest room is in disarray.
'Grandpa! We must have somewhere to play!'
In *their* toilet, things seem a little rum.
The seat is stuck down with chewing gum!
The toilet roll is much reduced in size.
What remains lies in folds upon the floor.
Was a cream puppy seen near the door?

My granddaughter is on the kitchen steps,
reaching up to the cupboard which I *had*
        designated *out of reach of children!*
'Grandpa …
why have you moved that huge biscuit tin
        where you keep all your lovely chocolate?

Grandpa?'
'Well?'
'May we come again? Soon?'
'Well … Yes …
yes, of course you may.
Now. Don't forget your pocket money …
and … chocolate.
Be sure to give your chewing gum
        to your lovely mum!'

Now they are gone, I can relax
and swear as much – as – I like!

Sophie B

So sharp!
   So bright!
Our instant delight.
Of love, so long deprived,
was it she who contrived …
not knowingly …
but with her natural charm,
to enter our hearts …
  to give us …
    endless …
      lasting joy?
Surrounded by our warmth,
    we pray …
      that one day …
She will forgive and forget …
the wretchedness
she will leave behind.

Voyage from the Mind

He learnt to sail
        on Barton Broad
        in Norfolk's fine county,
        where his hero Nelson
                learnt so many years before.

He cannot boast
        of great victories or successes,
        but he shares
        one thing in common
        with our naval Lord.
                He can *hold* a telescope
                        to his *blind* eye.

Although now with
        little sight or hearing,
        he can *look* into the mind
        and *listen* to the words
                as they begin to form and flow,
                        cascading from the memory.

The rich current
        is caught by his pen,
                aided by his magnifying glass.
Together they grapple
        with the flood of ideas.
He is often sucked into
        a whirlpool of words
                which hurl him
                        upon angry shores
which mock his disabilities.

Daring the slack tides
        of his thoughts,
he seeks again
        to make sense of the message
                from the mind.

He will never feel
        the adoration of the crowd
        as did his hero,
but he may become aware
        of the polite appreciation
        of his fellows
        and those lovely maidens
        who circle around him
                by the riverside.

The Messengers

He stands at the bus stop
        on a crisp March morning.
The sun offers a hint of warmth.

Dainty blossoms
        from the Prunis tree
        quickly cover his coat
        and the ground around him.

They whisper as they float by
        'Don't be afraid.
        We know you can
            hardly see us.
        We are not snowflakes
            but messengers of Spring.'

Waiting for the Mist to Clear

Waiting for the mist to clear.
The sun is near, so near, it is nearly here.
No breeze to baffle my hearing aids –
there's the cuckoo! So loud, so near, it is
       waiting for the mist to clear.

Yetminster Station is silently
       waiting for the mist to clear.
Diesel locomotive approaches cautiously
       waiting for the mist to clear.
Impatient passengers at Maiden Newton are
       waiting for the mist to clear.

In the gardens at Dorchester,
silent birds flit even more silently
from branch to branch, while they are
       waiting for the mist to clear.
The mist clings to the wire
and the nets of the tennis courts,
would-be Wimbledon aces are
       waiting for the mist to clear.

Suddenly, the sun is here, beaming everywhere!
Its brilliance pains my warped eyes.
A cooling breeze baffles my hearing aids.
Oh! To be a cuckoo, a train driver,
or even a tennis champion,
but no –

I must be content
and grateful for my friends,
so skilled with ears and eyes
who never fail me.
I thought of them this morning when they were
        waiting for the mist to clear.

First Love

My first love
      is the Spring morning,
            radiant in her
                  scarlet, crimson and gold.

Though …
      sometimes,
            she can be
                  sharp and cold.

As can any woman,
      I have been told!

Lovers Equinox (The Lure of Spring)

Winter stands astride the land
    and grips me with his icy hand.
His awesome breath tries to break my bones
    and saps my resolve to wait for Spring.
Surely, she must come soon?
Who else can move Winter from centre stage?
It seems so long since she sent her early messengers
    – pure, gentle snowdrop and exploding crocus.
Look! Look! Spring comes bustling from the wings.
Winter strikes back with lightning flash,
    thunder clap and stinging hail.
Undeterred, Spring pushes back the shrouds of night
    and kindles the lengthening day.
Then she sprinkles Winter's sombre cloak with her
    dainty, dancing golden-headed children.
Perplexed, Winter succumbs.
Even his hard heart is melting.
For who can resist a woman's warmth
    when we poor stallions are made for love?
And so, Winter's sharp and jagged pattern
    gives way to Spring's bright, colourful design.
The climbing sun titillates his thoughts
    as he greets his Lady Caroline.

May

The sun lifts
    bowed heads and hearts
        from long Winter's
            stress and tension.

Cuckoo's short song
    adds pleasure
        to the warm stillness
            of quiet evenings.

Daffodils and tulips
    have been overtaken by
        ceanothus' torrents of blue
            which are in friendly competition
                with the cascade of the pool.

Hanging baskets
    begin their journey
        to a frenzy of colour.

Begonia, fuchsia, marigold,
    petunia and busy lizzie
        have settled into
            their Summer homes
                of terracotta pots,
                    timber troughs
                        and fresh-dug borders.

Marauding cats,
    scolding blackbirds
        and lively goldfish
            all join in to make
                this busy month
                    the merriest of them all!

Ridgeway

As man first strode the Ridgeway
  it is still the same today.
Sharp flints beneath his tender feet
  soothed by the fragrant sweets of May.

The cuckoo calls across the trees,
  so certain of his welcome
  but man's thoughts hold a different focus
  as he strides, hunched,
against the bitter breeze.

The season is so late
  that longest day
  will soon pass through
  time's swinging gate
  and hurry on ahead.
Summer could be cold and wet,
to everybody's dread.

Next year, dear Spring,
you must do as you are told.
Come in on soft, warm breezes
  and not the bitter cold.

You will be followed
  by the juicy smell
  of new-mown hay
  and we shall share kind thoughts
  as we pass along this way.

The Bluebell Wood

The snowdrops and the catkins are sure proof
     that the shortest day has flown.

The crocuses in the slanting Winter sun
     bring colour to the bitter scene.

Mad March thrashes the daffodils.
The broken ones are fetched indoors
     to add joy to the lengthening day.

The pale primroses are quickly followed
     by the dainty cowslips
     to adorn the long-awaited threshold of Spring.

At the approach of May,
     a kind friend drives him to Bailey Ridge
     where the trees are busy making their new green canopies.

Beneath, as far as his eyes can tell,
     there is a carpet of blue,
     each tuft is colour-fast.

It is so perfect in its imperfection
     that no Persian hand, however skilled,
     could sew and weave to match.

He leans against a trunk
     embraced by the warm Spring breezes.

The cuckoo from Honeycomb Wood
     brings Delius to his side.

This is the pinnacle of his Spring.

There is much, much more to follow
    but nothing thrills him like this magic carpet.

The colour of its fabric is etched upon his memory.

A while later, a kind hand touches his arm.

His friend reminds him he must return
    to his land of telephones and stress.

He assures him they will return next year.

By then, should his eyes not detect this lovely blue,
the cuckoo will summon Delius
    who will take him firmly by the hand
    and guide him through this magic land.

Bumble Bee

A warm Spring day heralds your arrival.
In full flight you thud against the window.
It must hurt. I hold my head in sympathy.
Now you are raging against the conservatory roof of modern
    triple glaze.
The bright warm sun finds its way through but there is no
    way through for you.
It makes my heart ache to hear you thudding against the
    window again.

The patio doors are flung wide.
The warm air currents carry you back to the triple glaze.
You are incensed by the sun's unflinching stare.
I increase the volume of my hearing aids. You sound so angry.
I wonder if you are swearing with frustration as I do all day
    long?
I cannot see to usher you through the doorway of this your
    temporary hangar.
Why do you always try to leave at full throttle?

Where are you now? I hear no droning nor the prisoner's
    frenzied dance against the window pane.
To escape the sun's intensity you have dropped to recover
    upon the restful pattern of the cool tiles.
Have I found you? My magnifying glass will tell me.
I crouch. You are motionless.
The glass shows my withered eye the magnificence of your
    natural perfection which sends excited messages to my
    brain.
Without the glass, you are a smudge, a dirty mark upon the
    tile.

My partial sight would have passed you by without knowing
  you were there.
The glass reveals your tiny wings.
How do they lift you and then propel you at such speed?
My knees are sending an urgent message to my brain.
'Quick! Tell him to stand up straight and stop romancing.
He's not crouching in the gully or at point as he did for so
  many Summers long ago.
He must heed the signs of ageing.'

Stay still little friend. I will help you to regain your freedom.
A glass tumbler acts as a short-stay prison.
Across the cool tile I gently ease a postcard which tickles your
  undercarriage.
Your reaction is immediate, dramatic, violent.
In the doorway, the tumbler ends its brief commission.
Your radar eagerly embraces the warm breezes.
Straining wings tempt your clumsy lumberings into soaring
  flight.
Immediately, you are lost to the limit of my vision.
As I replace the means of freedom, I finger the postcard which
  was your air ticket, your launch pad.

You will return many times before the days grow cold again.
One day I will try to calm your blundering impatience and
  coax you to listen to the music which bears your name.

Battery Hen

I am in the warm and dry.
North wind does not pipe my eye.
Rain on the roof never bedraggled my feathers so fine
that I need to be hung out on an old clothes line.
Feather-bedded with plenty of food and water,
I never need to wear any sort of halter.
I'm not left in the dark.
This really is a lark!
Pity, pity, the poor old free-range hen,
if, for animal rights, you have a yen.
Out in the beastliest, cold winds and weathers,
it plays the very devil with their feathers.
In the cold and in the heat,
they scratch around to make ends meet.
Cooped-up, without any central heating.
My cosy home really takes some beating!
Worst of all, they are always at the behest
of that cockerel, who is such a bloody pest!
One little thing on their credit side
is something I really can't abide.
They do not have to sit
in this awful chicken shit.

Summer Afternoon

The climbing rose is flushed
      with warm, scented blossom
            which charms the nose.

The cascade chatters and chuckles
      its way into the pool,
where golden fish
      laze under round, green pads
            which are a platform
                  for a burst of colour.

Garden furniture is set for tea.
Female feet shed their shoes
      then sink with gratitude
            into soft, cool lawn.

Cups of tea – and cakes
      from the morning toil –
            prompt welcome nods of appreciation.

Gracious living!

Nothing disturbs the summer afternoon
      until – a wasp –
hovers near the jam–filled sponge!

Winter Evening

Neighbourliness

The house is in darkness.
The telephone in the hall
        rings three times.
He does not answer it,
but opens the door
        to admit his neighbour.

She leads the way
        into the warm room.
As he takes her cloak
        the flames from the inviting fire
leap in greeting.

They reveal that she is clad only
        in a brief, clinging, muslin wrap.

She lies on the settee.
He kneels down beside her …

Relaxation

He sits under the bank
      with his back to the sun
      watching the sparkling, clear water
      tumbling over the weir.

Brilliant dragonflies hover.
Bees drone. The cows
      tug at their green diet, nostrils blowing.
The laughter of children at play hurries across
      the fields to greet him.

Perch should start biting
      in half an hour or so.
They make a tasty supper.
In the early evening
      pike may come on to feed.
What a test of skill!
It is past eleven – time for coffee
      and to see what delights are in the lunch hamper.

Fishing is so relaxing!

He looks over his shoulder,
his rod nods, then bends,
he sees his float disappearing.
Perch have started biting early.

Coffee flask rolls down the bank!

Hurricane

The thunder cracks and cracks again.
Rabbits scurrying in our lane.
Look! Look! Here comes the rain.

The gathering storm was Sahara born.
In searing heat it kept its feet
        above the sand
                as it slowed across the land
                        to Atlantic's eastern strand.

Moving westward it gathered speed
        like a malevolent, angry steed,
then smashed itself with ease
        against the Florida Keys.

Leaving the New World with
        a trail of discontent,
it moved towards the Old
        before its strength was spent.

'We are in our Summer bowers
        of *village fetes* and *shows of flowers*,
                with *flags* and bunting-topped marquee,
where we do enjoy our cups of tea.'

This Hurricane of fancy name?
Is it Mabel
        that rumbles early
                down our lane?
Look! Look! Just look at that rain!

Leaves

Leaves sprouting
        adorned in their fresh Spring green
        as new clothing for majestic trees
        all so different yet each one formed to perfection
        enjoying the laughter of warm breezes
        hiding the homes of nesting birds
        offering shelter from the stormy skies
        giving welcome shade from the remorseless sun
        sodden by downpours
        retreating from the lash of storm–force winds
        dying – signalling approaching Autumn
        falling, gently, quietly, in the misty silence
        to weave fascinating carpets with differing shapes and
           brilliant hues.

Eased into rich earth by friendly worms, rejuvenated,
        they will sprout again in the Spring of a new year.

Raindrops

So still in the darkness … silent … menacing.
Uncertain eyes are open wide though they see no more
       than if they were squeezed tight shut!
Every forward step is a probe, fearful less it treads into nothingness
       then falling … falling … into a hell of broken bones.

But wait… listen, listen!
The sound of water … dripping … dripping.
Raindrops! Born of a leaden sky, lit by a brilliant rainbow
       which is clad in all the colours of the spectrum.
The raindrops first sights and sounds
       are lightning flashes and crackling thunder
       as they rush for the cover and protection of rich earth.

Filtering through, each one arrives crystal clear
       as it splashes upon the cavern floor.
Soon they will race each other to join a rivulet
       coursing into a mountain stream
       which cascades unflinching from towering heights
       in shimmering drapes of white,
even in the still of hot Summer days when shy creatures
       come to cool themselves in its spray.

Impatiently, it speeds on, to fall where salmon leap, into mighty
    river.
Easing its way past gentle herds and noisy flocks,
mighty river warms to the laughter of children at play
       and smiles to itself at the blissful nakedness of lovers
       so secure in the certainty of their concealment!

Fly fishermen stand in its shallows
>waving their rods as if they were magic wands
>and wait, so patiently, for salmon to snatch at tasty flesh
>only to be snared by Blue Charm or Lady Caroline.
Salmon's doom is angler's triumph!

Serene majestic river, ever confident of reaching its journey's end
>tends the needs of many travellers on its way.
Suddenly, the mood is changed
>as its smooth surface reflecting the silver light of the sun
>is ruffled, creased and scarred,
like silver paper discarded from a chocolate bar.

The sun is quickly overtaken by the chariots of the gathering storm
>and mighty river is engulfed by the predatory sea
>which, in turn, is commanded by the wind
>whose terrifying shrieks summon tumultuous waves,
>>foaming with anger
>as they pound the shore with the fists of mighty giants.

The wind proves its mastery
>as it reaps a ceaseless harvest of raindrops from the
>>captive sea.
The raindrops enjoy a reunion in the clouds
>until they must prepare to fall again, this time perhaps
>clad in the white coat of Winter to warm slumbering
>>earth
>or as harsh hail which violates gentle, innocent, Spring
>>blossom.

Autumn Leaves

Falling – in death
        they make carpets of rich colour
        only to be blanketed by November fogs,
then they sparkle with the tracery
        of frost in December.

Undisturbed by the festive clamour
        and the bells ringing in the new year
        they lie covered by January's silent snow,
soon to be washed by the rain
        that fills February's dyke.

Rough and ready March has so little time
        to complete its Spring-cleaning,
it hurls and twirls them out of its way.

Green grass, now free of their untidiness,
shakes off Winter's slumber
        and *grows* impatient to be mown.
Its pungent Spring juices titillate our nostrils
        and we leap for joy.

High above, the *deciduous* tree
        is *evergreen* once more.

October

When leaves fall from grace

Their end comes in October
       although they have given
       their lives to the tree.
They float, gently, quietly down
       without complaining
       having always lived
       in fear of sudden rejection.

The Mellow Season

The climbing rose
    still stoutly wears its blooms
    though nights grow long
    and mornings chill.

Gusty breezes bring warnings
    of worse to come.

Soon sorrowing petals
    fall as tears
    and are swept away.

Pruned and cleaned,
    the rose will sleep
    until touched by Spring.

Summer Gloom

It descends towards
      the end of June.
The longest day
      has gone so soon.

The waning harvest moon
      spurs images of
            Winter's harsh comforts,
                dark, joyless days.

Long black nights
      incessant rain,
            chill winds,
                sharp frost
                    and who knows –
                        when it snows?

The shortest days
      are graced
            by the festive season
            of good will
                which brings relief.

Then, when all seems bleak,
      thoughts seek evidence
            of Spring's early messenger.
                In the dank, dead,
                    January hedge
                        the catkin
                            dangles so cheekily.

Feeling is Seeing

Lack of sight brings you
        into ever sharper focus.
Sensitive hands are eager
        to serve as eyes.
Feeling is Seeing!

Desire does not seek rapacious love
but a gracious, gentle–caring–caressing.

As we lie, our thoughts will soar
        to the very ceiling of our minds,
bursting to tell, but remaining ever silent.

Colourfast

What is colour to a blind man?
Her colour is in her breath, her voice –
     the touch of her hand,
each time it surges through him
       like the fire in neat whisky.

The memory – and – the anticipation
of her voice over the telephone,
the fleeting warmth of her thigh
in the timbered restaurant
     pilots him through
        his endless twilight days.

She gave him
     the will to live.
Instinctively, he knows
     they will be together
        until the very end
          of time.

You

You, as you are
      my shining star.
      You took my words
      into your mouth
      and offered me
      luxurious sounds
      unheard before
      by my aided ears.

My eyes could not see you.
I had never clasped your hand in greeting
      nor brushed your lips with mine.
I had not felt your breath
      nor held your warmth.

Yet, in reality,
my words and your mouth
      were as one for ever
      beyond eternity, into infinity.
The ebb and flow of your voice
      trickled over me as I lay
      on the shore of the paradise
      of which only we were aware.

Love

Love so constant
    yet not possessive.

Love so eager
    yet so restrained.

Love so warm
    yet not demanding.

Love so longing
    yet so patient.

Love so true
    yet never fulfilled.

Orbit

Ravishing, dark, dark hair,
      sparkling eyes,
            infectious laughter,
                revealing
                     a sense of humour
                          laced with fun
                              and warmth.
One day, perhaps,
      kisses may be welcomed.

In the meantime,
      what boundless joy
            to lie
                within her orbit.

Clandestine Meeting

The porch light shines
on door ajar.
Paradise may not be far.
In fleeting seconds …
a glimpse of flimsy frills
finger to pursed lips, urges silence
porch light extinguished
door lock clicks
foot fall in hall
tender greeting
soft hands caress warm cheeks.
Paradise beckons …

Weddings

Hope nothing goes wrong.
Don't say that!

Nice hat! Pink!
Made the boys wink.
One or two of the men
took note for sure.
She had a really nice two-piece
for the ceremony and didn't she
look good in that striking number
she wore to the party in the evening?!
Attractive woman!
Lovely trim figure. Nice bottom!
The bridegroom's mother … Was she?!
One of the pages complained about
his winged collar. Sore neck.
The other one fell in a puddle.
Puddle? Yes. A huge one.
Absolutely soaked. Poor little chap.
Did it rain then … ? Rain!
It rained – and rained – and rained.
Lovely wedding though.
Perfect …
Everything went like clockwork.
Did one of the men make off with
that lovely pink hat?
Yes. She had to redeem it.
Lucky man!
What a party in the evening!
What a day!
Lovely wedding … Lovely.

The Librarian

Neat, polite, objective.
Bright, impish eyes shelter
        behind gold-framed spectacles.

Cheeky freckles
        teased by a lock
                of unruly auburn hair ...
                        speak volumes.

Gentleness

Gentleness is what I sought
      away from the heat and strife
      of daily life
      which was so fraught.
Since my ears and eyes
      were muted
      I have found
      a gentler frame of mind.

Stop rushing about!
Do not shout
      and point the finger!
Learn to linger.
Stay still.
Be quiet.
Relax!

Forget the fax,
the car,
the train,
the aeroplane.
Be gentle and polite!

Those around you
      will respond to your smile
      with parting words
      of gentleness.

The Diamond Merchant

It became a habit
        to take his selfish pleasure
        from the perfectly formed little gems
        as they trickled through his hands,
without caring about their destiny.

Then as he was strolling
        the greying paths of life,
he was captivated by the
        queen-empress of them all.
        Instinctively, he knew he would
        never take possession of her.
Yet, she would invade
        his every thought and dream
        throughout eternity.

Opportunity Lost

He may have been handsome,
tall and straight of eye,
but did you his parents spy?
Age-withered, stooped, sullen eye, rasping voice.
Seek not disagreement with your choice.
It is to be preferred to a life, perhaps,
tainted by reluctant indifference.

Be patient now.
Look around.
Prepare the ground
      where, surprisingly,
rich treasures may be found.

Settling down, is not for
      every maiden – dark or fair.
Though, should a treasure come your way,
embrace her until your dying day
      and live a life of eager happiness.

Should that treasure not be found,
life will still abound
      with ecstasy and joy of giving.
Listen to what the sages say!
If they could again live their day
      or have time allowed for such,
they would have enjoyed
      at least …
      twice as much!

An opportunity lost is but a door to a vista flushed with
unimagined opportunities yet to be discovered.

Bus Stop

He stands alone, anticipating her arrival.
Her smiling greeting is never diminished
      despite the chiding of the weather.
It gives him joy and warms him like a flask
      in the dark, damp chill of that early morning.
She is highly intelligent, so placid, almost withdrawn,
yet with a teasing sense of humour.
If it were not so dark their eyes would embrace
      as in the gentle quiet of a Spring evening.
The touch of her hand makes him ponder.
Does she long to escape – occasionally –
      from her daily round?
Home-to-bus-to-office-to-bus-to-home.
His thoughts turn to kissing her rich, red lips.
They are both mature, with experience
      of the greying paths of life.
Would the meeting of their tongues
      release her from the restraints of convention,
revealing an eager tigress,
ready to respond to his warm embrace?
Will his thoughts offend her?
If not, how soon can they be together – alone?

Girl Green

Brunette. Perfectly made.
Even more so, it seemed,
when tanned by the Summer sun.
Articulate. Intelligent. Sharp of eye.
Considerate. Determined. Thoughtful.
Warm sense of humour.
Declared enemy of all injustice.
Completely at ease in company
      and conversation with anyone.
Tinkling, infectious laugh.
Blessed with real charisma.
So magnetic.
With her sense of adventure and zest for life,
it came naturally to live dangerously.
She was strongly attracted to men
     and pursued, relentlessly, by them
        as they were captivated by her aura.

When displeased. No sound.
Her look terrified.

Dreaming

Grandpa Brian is not at home today,
he is at least a million miles away.
… Floating …
Gloating – over his hordes of money
       or simply eating bread and honey.
Snoring – in his garden chair – so gently,
perhaps he's dreaming of his Bentley.
Shall we telephone his next of kin
       or put it down to too much gin?!

Values

In the Bentley
     there is plenty
         of room.
Father bought it
     in the boom.

The collapse of
     share prices
         meant he gave up
          all his vices
            except

               the Bentley
               which he drives
               so gently.

The Room

The door is small
      though the walls are tall.
The ceiling is new.
It is painted blue
like the sky
      where the angels live,
who will care for me
      when I die.

Now …
      while I am still very small
      if I learn to jump
         really high,
I may reach that sky
      where the angels live,
who will care for me
      when I die.

With my grandson in mind.

The Seeker

Death, where are you?
I am your willing companion.
While I wait for you
      to answer my plea,
patience must hold my hand.

Shall I seek
immortality or damnation?
The one may cost me dear.
The other is always near.

Longing

Yes, I have gone …
but, I am near.
You, can still sense me.
I am close to you.
Hold on to me
in your memories.
Times …
    merge into …
        one deep longing …
          to be together …
            always … !
Never, to be wrenched apart.

Badock Hall, University of Bristol, 9 July 2006.
Written during the playing of *Elegy* by Gabriel Fauré. Played by Raymond Warren, Professor of Music (piano) and Geoffrey Palmer, Doctor of Music (cello).

'My mention of Raymond Warren reminded me of "Longing". The longing which comes with bereavement. It was spontaneous. I love the cello – it just grabs me – and there I was, sketching and writing as fast as I could!

Much of what I write is like that. Something captivates one of my senses – and away I go! Often in the small hours. I wake – I must note it down. If I neglect to do so, the mind closes a door. No matter how hard I try, it is quite impossible to open.'

Football

It is *not* allowed in the hall
      or indoors at all.
Neither upstairs *nor* down.
See them frown!

Not one smile
      even when I'm quiet
      for a little while –
         … until …
              I start to play again.

Aunt Jane loves me more than most.
I play the host
      when she comes to tea
      even though I know
      there may not be
      a *single* cream cake for me.

   With my grandson in mind.

Cricket

True wicket.
Easy cricket.

When it was green
      it seamed
            like a dream.

When it was
      dry and crumbly
            it suited my spin.

I used to grin
      when I watched the batsmen
            roll about like sailors
                  in a force eight.

I think I took nine,
      or was it ten?

How their hearts sank
      as I made them
      walk the plank!

      With my grandson in mind.

Hospital

Do not dread
    being put to bed.
In the theatre
    you may see pictures
    even though you sleep so sound.
Lions and tigers can abound.
You will wake up feeling sore
    but there's a lovely meal in store.
Perhaps you'd like a nice hot drink?
That pretty, freckled nurse; did she wink?

Cor! What a laugh
    if she would help you with your bath.
You could undo the ribbon
    which ties her lovely auburn hair
    and watch it fall – just
    as far as possible!

Now then, remember, in the morning
    to heed the surgeon's warning.
You must take it easy!

The Hospital Bed

It is said the hospital bed
       will be comfortable if you can
              watch it being made by that
                     cheeky young nurse.

Some would say the one
       with the nicely *rounded* figure.

Then in it you lie expecting
       to be tended by her ... But no,
              it is the Ward Sister!

You have to lie quite still
       while she examines your ill.
'Where does it hurt?'
'Just down *there*, nurse.'
That makes matters worse.
She prods it extra hard
       to remind you she is the Ward Sister.
Now it is very sore.
Pins and needles galore.
Major surgery for sure.

The lovely cheeky young nurse
       comes to take your blood pressure,
              pulse and temperature – Ooooh!
They all went sky high,
       just like flying a kite.
The Ward Sister came to check the readings.
They dropped like a stone.

I'm feeling much better after the surgery
        and keep looking out for that
                lovely, cheeky young nurse ...

Eh! ... What's that. ...?
She's been moved downstairs
        to the geriatric men's ward!
My goodness me, they could be in
        for a record number of
                heart attacks and seizures!

It must be in the best interests
        of the management to lock away
                all their motorized walking frames,
otherwise they will be chasing her
        up and down the ward!
Can you imagine the jam?
That ward has not yet
        been fitted with traffic lights!

Easter

East makes the name.
Easter Day breaks dull and cold.
The East wind blows chill.
East, lies Calvary,
      that Spring of hope.
            Did He die in vain?

Corruption in all its guises
      is our shame.
See the halt, the blind, the lame.
Soon we shall embrace the second millennium
      weighed down by the chains of
            Bosnia – Chechnya – Dunblane.
            It has always been the same.

Resurrection

How long before the eye drops
      smite the devil in my eye?
How long will the devil's cruel nails
      hold me to his blackest cross?
Could Gethsemane be worse than this?

I had accepted partial sight.
Then, if I woke in the night
      I knew the signs of approaching day.
Now, the brightest dawn is lost to me.
Twilight is as far as I can see.

Has Spring, my favourite season, stayed away?
Her children seem bewildered
      as I pass them by.
At the prompting of a companion
      I stoop to caress them.
My unseen tears mingle
      with the dew on their petalled heads.

My white cane is my eye.
How deep the kerb, how steep the step?
The road is now too wide.
It holds perils unseen,
as frightening as a fast flowing river.
I must wait to be ferried across.
Perhaps St Christopher will carry me over?
   I cannot shop, or write – or read.
When I meet a friendly greeting
      I strain to see the face
            which detracts from conversation.
So my response is often muted.

At home I hold the telephone with ease.
The kitchen, which I know so well
      is quite a pleasant sort of hell
Now … Shall I have another drink?
No … I'll pour it down the sink.
I must never give way.
(Surely, He has not forsaken me?)
      I long for *My* Easter Day.

Dual Sensory Loss

No speeding train
or shooting star,
      only the breeze.

No owl's hoot
or vixen's cry,
      only sharp frost.

No friendly greeting
or 'What is yours?'
      only wood-smoke.

No impatient horn
or raucous shouts,
      only pungent fog.

No lights on beam
or screeching brakes,
      only the pain …

Profound Deafness

As the advancing years
    bring fears
    of the beckoning vault,
Could the gloom
    of the tomb
    hold such frightening silence?

No sound of the whispering breeze
    through the trees,
    rustling the curtains.
No vixen's scowl
    in response
    to screeching owl.
No cough, nor snore.
No slamming door.
No lash of rain on window pane.
No rumble of thunder
    to disturb the slumber.
No creaking stair
    as maiden fair
    meets lecher, unaware
    of his planned rendezvous.
No alarm clock
    sweet dreams to block.
No church clock chime
    to signal waking time.
No eight o'clock pips
    to disturb her lips.
No song of a bird
    can be heard.

No milk bottle clinks
as the milkman winks
        at warm silks.
No footsteps
        or high heels, clicking.
No morning greeting.

No sound of
        the happiness of children at play,
        nor the rustling newspaper
        as it falls in disarray.
No crackling logs.
No dripping tap.
No letterbox flap
        to disturb a nap.
No postman's rat-tat.
        Nothing like that.

No egg shells breaking
        before the baking.
No sound of egg whisk
        in basin it frisks.
No wooden spoon
        pastry bowl ringing.
No boiling egg.
No silver spoon in cup or saucer.
No whip-crack of sheets
        on a roaring
        March morning.

No cockerel's reveille.
No clucking hen.
No damn pigeons.
No pigs in pen.
No horses' hooves.
No bleating sheep.

No lowing meadow ladies.
No clamouring geese.
　　　(what a feast
　　　at Michaelmas.
　　　What shall we do
　　　with all that grease?)
No swinging gate.
No racing brook.
No plunging waterfall.
No cat.
　　　Oh! Think of that.
No bark.
No lark
　　　on high
　　　in the sky.

No noise
of
aircraft
children's toys
motorbike
or car
horn
or screeching brakes
radio
or telephone
nor voices
of
newspaper boys.

Spellbound

Her long dark hair
and eyelashes
which seem
to sweep right up
      to heaven
hold him
      in a trance
as the petals
      of the deep
            red rose
               of love
                  dance
                     before his eyes

The Old Enemy

It arrives without any warning.
       Cautiously –
              he leaves his bed.

The ceiling is too close.
The door avoids him.
He encounters hurricane force 10
       along the landing.
He sits on the toilet.
The window moves towards him.
He shuts his eyes.
The end of the world
       is only seconds away.

Nausea overtakes him.
All plans for the day
       are so disappointed.

No washing, shaving,
       dressing or eating.
He will have to stand, sit or lie
       in as much comfort
       as Labyrinthitis will allow,
       but it is so treacherous.

He must be patient
       and wait for it to retreat.

Autumn '39 and '40

Those of us who are now in
the Autumn of our lives,
remember another Autumn when
on a brilliant sunny Sunday morning
a voice from the wireless set told us
we were at war with Germany.

This was the voice of a man
who was much despised by our fathers.
Soon we were to hear from the same wireless set
the sonorous tones of a man who exhorted us
to cherish the freedom we knew and loved.
This voice made our fathers smile
and warmed their hearts.
This man was in the Autumn of his life
yet, undaunted, he took on the whole world
and through that same wireless set
we never doubted the outcome.

The next Autumn we watched *The Few*
playing the game of death
in the clear, blue sky.
The awesome sounds of battle,
the victor's vapour trails,
the vanquished, enveloped
in a plume of smoke,
then a belch of flame.

Seeing what *The Few* could do
although only armed with our gas masks,
we spared no thoughts for jack boots
but devoted ourselves to eke out
our sweet ration of bull's-eyes and sherbet fountains.

Events have proved us right as we are
still here in the Autumn of our lives,
although we are horrified to find that
our penny sherbet fountain now costs over *half-a-crown*.
It seems to us that there is not so much sherbet.
The liquorice doesn't taste so good
as that we were forbidden to eat in bed
which, as we fell asleep,
stuck to our ears and the pillows!

V.E. Day Remembered – Fifty Years On

When they were in their youth
they were sharp of ear and eye,
competitive, industrious, with zest for life.
All of fifty years gone by.

Each one now seventy or more.
Still paralyzed, or blind, or deaf,
or without hands, or feet.
Fifty care-worn years are their reward.

A bride – in utility white – serene.
Such were young hopes and dreams,
but she turned away from the bed-bound wreck,
leaving him alone for fifty endless years.

Missing, presumed killed in action.
His youthfulness is in the faded photograph
she still holds most dear, even though
she has outlived the fiftieth anniversary.

Victor and vanquished embrace today
exchanging memories of their battlefield.
Then they look with horror at *Sarajevo* –
fifty years on.

The Agonies Of Parting

The newborn child from its mother's breast.
The first day at school,
    leaving mother at the gate.
The child, nurtured with every loving care,
    when the look on the surgeon's face
    tells that all his skills were not enough.
A beloved niece, unfortunately through brain cancer,
    which began with breast cancer.
What devilry is this?
Those perfectly formed fountains of life,
    which were such a haven
    and source of pointed pleasure.
She who was so beautifully made.
The death of one's first love
    though was of natural disaster.
Being forsaken for a new beau.
Sad memories of terminal illness
    of fond grandparents, aunts, uncles.

In old age, his circle would dwindle
    to just a few.
He will weep in secret.
Then he will embrace with his love,
    those of the younger wider circle.
Teaching them to store away memories
    of happy time they share together.
This will act as a warm cushion
    against the agonies which are certain
    to overwhelm them.

Death

Death stalks us
    day by day,
        by the hour and minute,
           even by the second,
it beckons.

Dog bite,
    cat's claw.
Lightning strikes –
    chimney tall –
        or golf club small.

High wind claims
    giant beech tree.
It takes anyone near by
    crashing into eternity.

Luckless infant,
    reckless youth,
        malignancy in prime,
           old age – at any time.

Car driven too fast.
Was the railway signal at danger?
Ship's red distress flare
Aircraft's May Day.
Its aptly named black box.

Civil strife
    sniper's bullets –
        genocide.

We have witnessed
        death's harvest being enriched
            with Aids, drugs
                and the ceaseless toil
                    of his arch-disciple,
                        the terrorist.

Whatever my end may be,
        I pray that
            the Silent Helmsman
                will steer me safely
                    across the Sea of Agony
                        to the Land of Peace.

Life and Death by the River

Restrained by their mothers' hands they watched the river with
      awe through the railings of the bridge.
After school, they chased each other along the path by the river.
In the holidays, they fished in the shallows, then, when they were
      bored they trailed their bare feet in the river.
He worked on the estate which ran down to the river,
      she nursed at the hospital which overlooked the water.
In the warm Summer twilight they made love
      on the soft grassy bank of the river.
They were married in the church whose yard edged the water.
From the church steps which lapped the water
      they were rowed along the river to their reception.
Their still-born baby was delivered in that same hospital.
She refused the flowers he had picked so lovingly by the river
      and kept staring out of the hospital window at the water
      with eyes sore from *wishing*.
On his way home to their riverside cottage he laid the flowers
      on the water one by one and watched them drift slowly
         away.
Each day when he arrived home he found her staring at the river.
When the ice thawed her body was taken from the water.
He was found hanging from the railing of the bridge.
His bare feet were trailing in the river.

The Empty Glass

A short while ago
    it was charged
    with amber cheer
    which warmed sagging thoughts.

It was firmly grasped
    by the hand
    that now lies still.

No more,
    to feel,
    or touch.

It is colder
    than the silent
    empty glass.

The Call to Arms

The days are long.
The nights are even longer.
Patience is the watchword –
an acquired steel – so flexible,
in such demand throughout
each and every timeless hour,
whatever the slings and arrows.

He can just make out the snow
with his warped eyes at two-o-three.
Through his hearing aids
he listens to the rain at four-and-twenty.
The wind moans at twenty-to-five
or is it twenty past?

Once she leaves their bed
she does not return;
but, rambling in her mind,
conducts an uncertain tour
upstairs and down
until it is breakfast time.
She is wearing three skirts today.
Was it three or four jumpers yesterday?
She has to be helped at the toilet.
She cannot bath or dress.
The fun they shared so many years ago
as he undressed her
is now an endless chore.

Her genius eclipsed all
who strayed within her firmament.
Her accomplishments were endless.

Suffice to say, her artistry was such
that she was at ease with each and every medium –
acrylic, charcoal, oil, pastel, pen and ink,
pencil or water colour.

Her skill and pleasure as a teacher
is acknowledged in letters from former pupils.

He will keep her garden as a shrine to her memory.
Perhaps she was at her brilliant best
in her paintings of individual flowers.

The art room is still,
her brushes and paints
wait unheeded
to be coaxed into life.
Her coveted garden shed
is now opened by his gardener.

Her gleaming Traveller stands in the garage,
free from rain, dust and mud.
This constant companion for thirty years
is locked – the key is hidden
lest she harms herself, or others.

The front door, too, is kept locked
to prevent her from escaping,
unsuitably clad in rain, shine,
or into the darkness.

Where is her coffee mug?
Her dessert spoon was in the pocket of her bed-jacket.
Her real nightdress was found,
tucked away, neatly folded,
inside his pillowcase.

As he wearily thrust his feet
down the bed last night,
his toes touched the missing plate.
Will you bathe her eyes, please?
Her eye shadow was her lipstick,
applied with her toothbrush.
Her coffee mug was hidden away
behind her dressing table.

Then their carer came,
armed with a flawless patience.
Her warmth enveloped them both.
She gave him leave to sleep
but he found none.
He lay wondering why
He in *His* perfect scheme of things
had decreed an end
so sad and tragic
for one so gifted.

Her body held a brimming reservoir
of mental and physical energy.
Now she is a drained and empty wasteland,
locked in the cruel and ever-tightening embrace
of Lewy Body.

Why does he not desert
his bride of forty years?
He married her
        for better, for worse,
        for richer, for poorer,
        in sickness and in health.
He does not forsake all others
for now, more than ever,
he needs their love.

Despite the lack of sleep
        he must answer the call to arms
        until the bitter end, although
        he knows there is no hope of victory.

Cruel Fate

An invasion
     of her brain and mind
     which increased for more than ten
     long, sad and tragic years.
She did not understand
     but did she know?
He watched her disintegration,
     her genius – withering away.
He lived through a daily agony
– did she?

Possession

She is lost …
The cruel monster
has devoured her brain.
She has shrunk away,
     but her genius
     is spread around
     for all to see.
That He can never
     take away from me.

Bereavement

She has gone.
No. She is there
       on the stair.
In the bathroom
       washing her hair.
Opening her lingerie drawer.

Her cheery greeting
       as she comes through
       the front door.

Always busy in the garden,
       secateurs in her gloved hand.
Her roses glowed
       on any exhibition stand.

Her paint brushes
       are waiting
       to be charmed into life.
Quiet and still
       lies her palate knife.

He slides his foot
       to her side of the bed.
It is cold.

She *has* gone.
No! … No! …
She will *always* be there …
       On the stair …

Homecoming

The house is in darkness.
He switches on the lights
     and moves slowly
     from room to room.

She is here,
on every chair,
by every door.
She touches each
     plate, dish and glass
     that he holds.
There is a silence everywhere.

As long as he lives there
     so will she.
When he leaves
     they will go together.

All Saints', Sutton Bingham

Fashioned nine centuries since
by those conscious of their art
and of their Maker.
Aged now with memories far
of cold and heat, wet and drought,
of joyous things to talk about.

Sadness? … Oh! … Yes! …
Much sadness along the way.
Plague, war, pestilence, vandalism, greed,
for such beautiful things they had no heed.
It has always been the same,
they followed each other down the lane.
Yet, despite the sword and shout,
It warms to those who find *It* out.

The saddest time of all?
In recent years the cottages
were submerged by the reservoir.
Their families had to move away.
The water was not for them
but for the townsfolk who lived nearby,
who neither knew nor cared nor heard their cry.

Although so old,
It is bright of face
and is being refreshed,
before *It* sets out
to greet the *third* millennium.
Tonight, in a changing world,
we witness a fragment
that has never changed.

We are lit by candles
as for centuries past.
I pray something of this flickering scene
may stay with you.

Some of you will come again.
Perhaps, alone, to stay a while,
to reach out – to touch and feel
Its timeless serenity,
for *It is a very special place*,
this beautiful, peaceful little church,
dedicated to All the Saints
at Sutton Bingham.

Why here?
Some talk of
uninterrupted lines of thought,
untouched by wind or rain.
Perhaps it was a compass point
determined by an unseen hand
that fixed this plot of land.

The Saxons made a tiny mark
but you, the Normans, came to stay
because you sent your ships away.

You built it strong and stout
to keep all sorts of evil out.
Who were you that fashioned it?
Were you dark and strict,
or blue and fair,
with a halo in your hair?
And is it true
you laid the maidens bare?

You were the victors.
What of the vanquished?
Were you hard on them
and took away every tiny gem?

The wall paintings?
Did they speak to you
as your skill gave such
form and face?
The light was poor.
How did you see
to paint them with such grace?

Then came the priest,
Oh! So full of care,
      because, you see,
           he had
                two Lords
                   to bear.

One was never far away.
The other was there,
up in the air, somewhere.
I often wonder
how he coped with them.
                Amen!

Churchyard

In the warm twilight
of the hot summer's day
    the air is still.

The claxton of the speeding train
hangs in the void
of the silver rails
which, having taken the strain,
    now lie still.

All good children
have gone scrubbed to bed.
    At last, their tongues are still.

Cars have stopped roaring
along the causeway.
It seems empty
    and at a stand still.
The herd, no longer lowing,
now ruminates as it lies so still.
    Even the roosting birds keep still.

The courting couple along the lane
are gently parked in his back seat bower,
the giggling died away within the hour,
    now all seems very still.

Teased all day
by the feathered casts
of the anglers at play,
the trout, now left alone
in the depths of the reservoir
    are still.

Its waves cease to be slaves
of the gusty breezes,
since the cast of darkness
has netted them
        and held them still.

The yachts on the landing slip,
with sails snug in canvas jackets
after a day
of enthusiastic straining
against Nature's power,
        are still.

Even the twinkling stars
        seem to be still.

The only sound
        is the beating
                of my heart,
                        because it feels so close to heaven.

Haste

What fools we are when young.
So eager for the sound of the gun
      to start the race of life.

So soon, we have
too much time
      for reflection,
           recrimination,
      and so many regrets.

The Future

Let us not be afraid!
We must have
the courage
to endure,
whatever
lies in store.

Entreaty

of an ordinary country boy

Never place me on a pedestal
       lest you destroy me.
Find me as I am,
       not as you would shape me.
Heed not my faults,
       but love me, always.

Epitaph

Genius? Speak not so wild!
    I am Friday's Child.
    Loving – Giving.
    An ordinary boy
        with joy of country living.